6 FAMOUS
PANCHATANTRA
STORIES

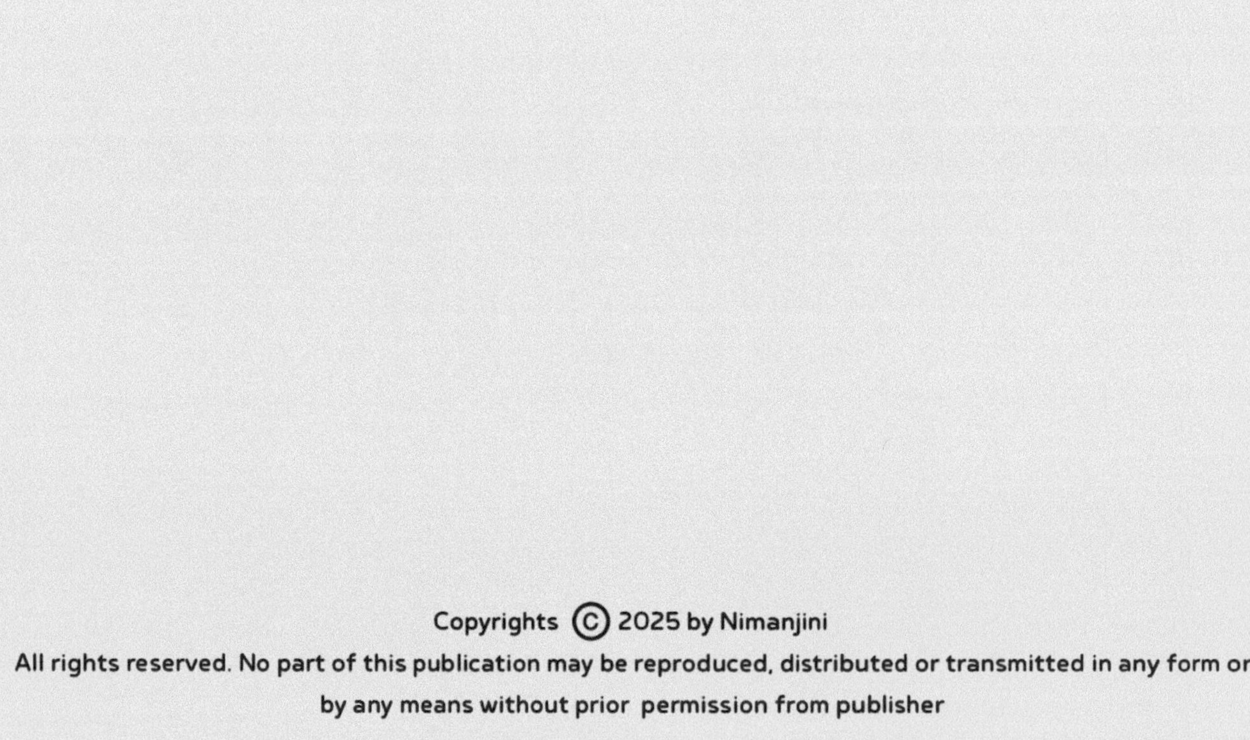

This book belong to

____

TABLE OF CONTENTS

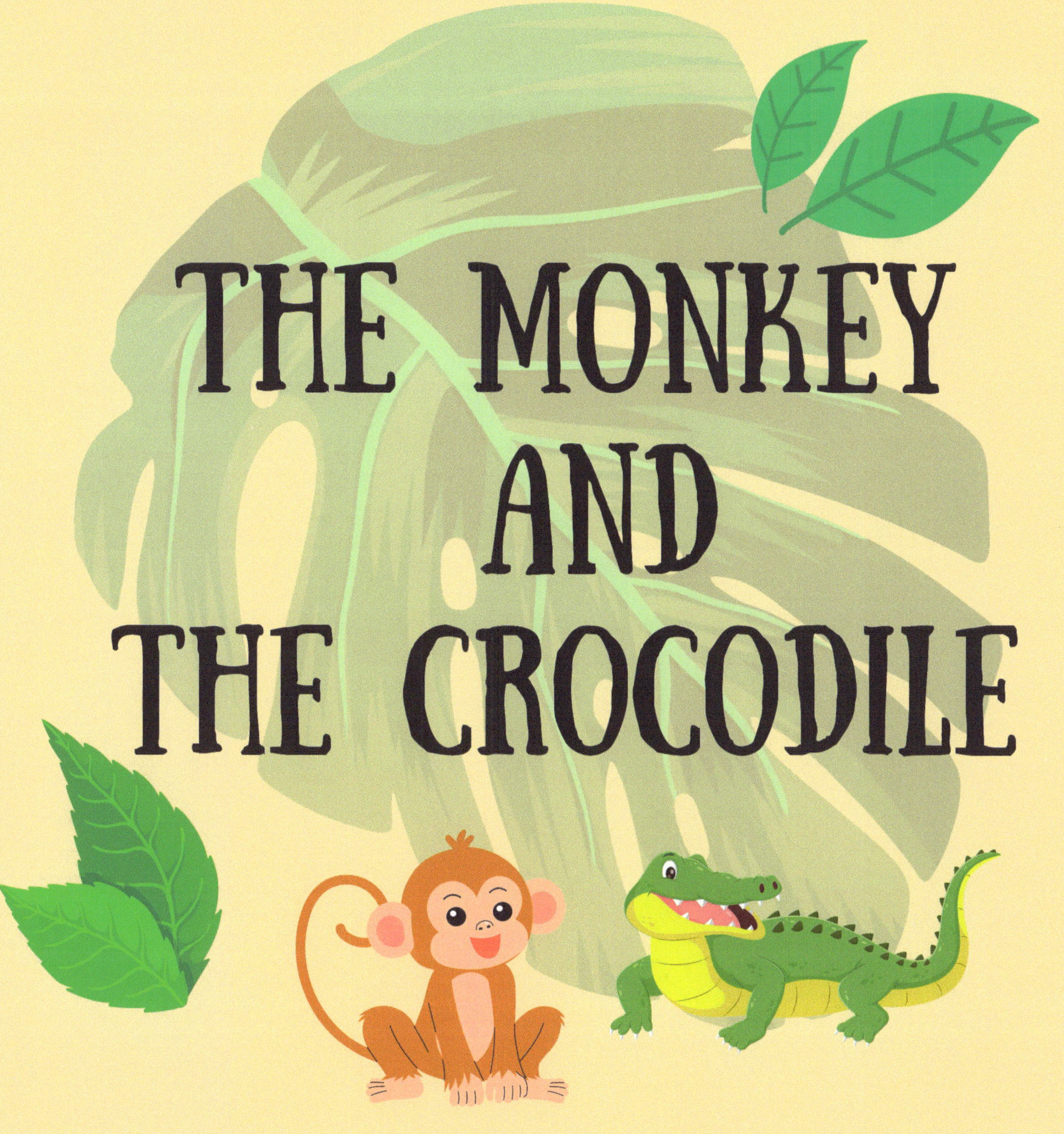

THE MONKEY
AND
THE CROCODILE

Once upon a time, in a dense jungle, there lived a clever monkey, on a big tree, near the river.

The tree bore sweet, juicy fruits and the monkey spent his days happily eating them.

One day, a crocodile
swam up to the
tree.He looked weak
and hungry.

Seeing this, the kind hearted monkey offered him some fruits. The crocodile was delighted.

The crocodile started visiting the monkey every day. Over time, they became good friends.

However, the crocodile's wife was greedy and jealous. She wanted to eat the monkey's heart, believing it would be as sweet as the fruits that he eats.

She said to her husband:

The crocodile was troubled, but he foolishly agreed.

The next day, he told the monkey:

The monkey, trusting his friend, climbed onto the crocodile's back.

As they reached the middle of the river, the crocodile blurted out:

The clever monkey thought of a plan.

The foolish crocodile believed him and swam back to the tree. The moment they reached the shore, the monkey leaped to safety and climbed, high up onto the branches of the tree.

You betrayed my trust, Crocodile! You were never my true friend. I will never make the mistake of trusting you again!

Feeling ashamed, the
crocodile swam away,
realising he had lost a
good friend forever.

MORAL OF THE STORY

A TRUE FRIEND IS SOMEONE WHO VALUES YOU AND NOT SOMEONE WHO DECEIVES YOU FOR THEIR OWN GAIN.

BEING CLEVER AND HAVING THE PRESENCE OF MIND CAN HELP OVERCOME EVEN THE MOST DIFFICULT SITUATIONS.

THE JACKAL
AND
THE DRUM

In a dense forest, a hungry jackal, roams in search of food. Days of wandering leaves him weak and he fears he might not find any food to eat.

As he walks through the jungle, he suddenly hears a loud, strange sound. Startled, he freezes in fear, wondering if danger is nearby.

The jackal cautiously follows the sound, his heart pounding. He wonders if a fearsome animal is making the sound. Should he run or investigate? His curiosity wins and he moves forward, step by step, towards the source of the booming sound.

The jackal finally finds a large drum lying on the ground. The wind was making the branches of the trees to strike the drum and cause the sound. The jackal realises that there is no danger and that his fear was unfounded.

Bravely, the jackal taps the drum with its paw. The hollow object makes another loud sound. He now realises that it was harmless.

He laughs at himself for being scared of something so simple. His courage helped him uncover the truth.

As the drum was of no use
to him, he turns around.
Nearby, he finds some food,
left by the hunters.

He eats to his hearts content realising that fear and hesitation could have kept him from discovering this opportunity.

MORAL OF THE STORY

FEAR OFTEN COMES FROM THE UNKNOWN. IF WE INVESTIGATE SITUATIONS CALMLY AND LOGICALLY, WE CAN OVERCOME FEARAND REACH THE GOAL.

THE BRAHMIN
AND
THE THREE THIEVES

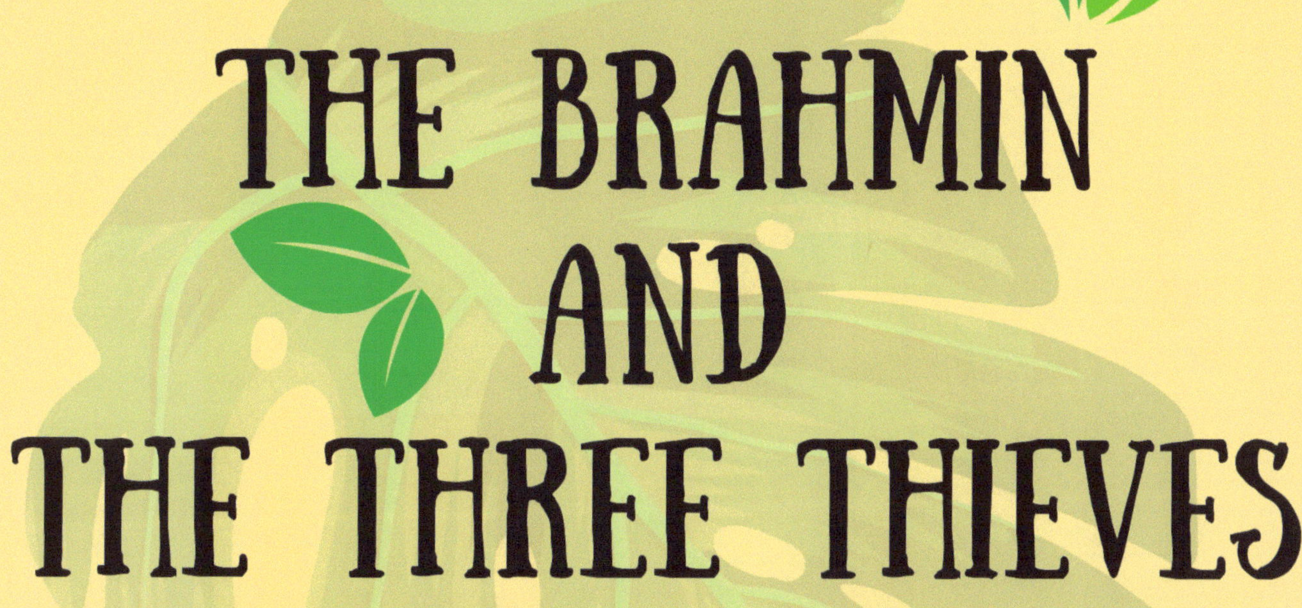

Once upon a time, a kind and wise
Brahmin used to perform religious
rituals in the village.

One day he received a goat as a
reward for performing the ritual.

Carrying the goat on his shoulders, he started his journey home, feeling happy and greatful. Three cunning thieves spotted the Brahmin carrying the goat. They knew they couldnot take the goat by force. So they came up with a trick to deceive him. They decided to approach him one by one and make him doubt his own eyes.

The first thief approaches the Brahmin and says

The Brahmin is surprised but ignores the thief, believing him to be a fool. He continues walking.

The second thief approaches the
Brahmin and says

The Brahmin gets confused. Could it be
that he was mistaken? Doubt begins to
creep into his mind, but he decides to
move on.

The third thief meets the Brahmin and exclaims!

Now fully convinced that some
thing is wrong, he panics.

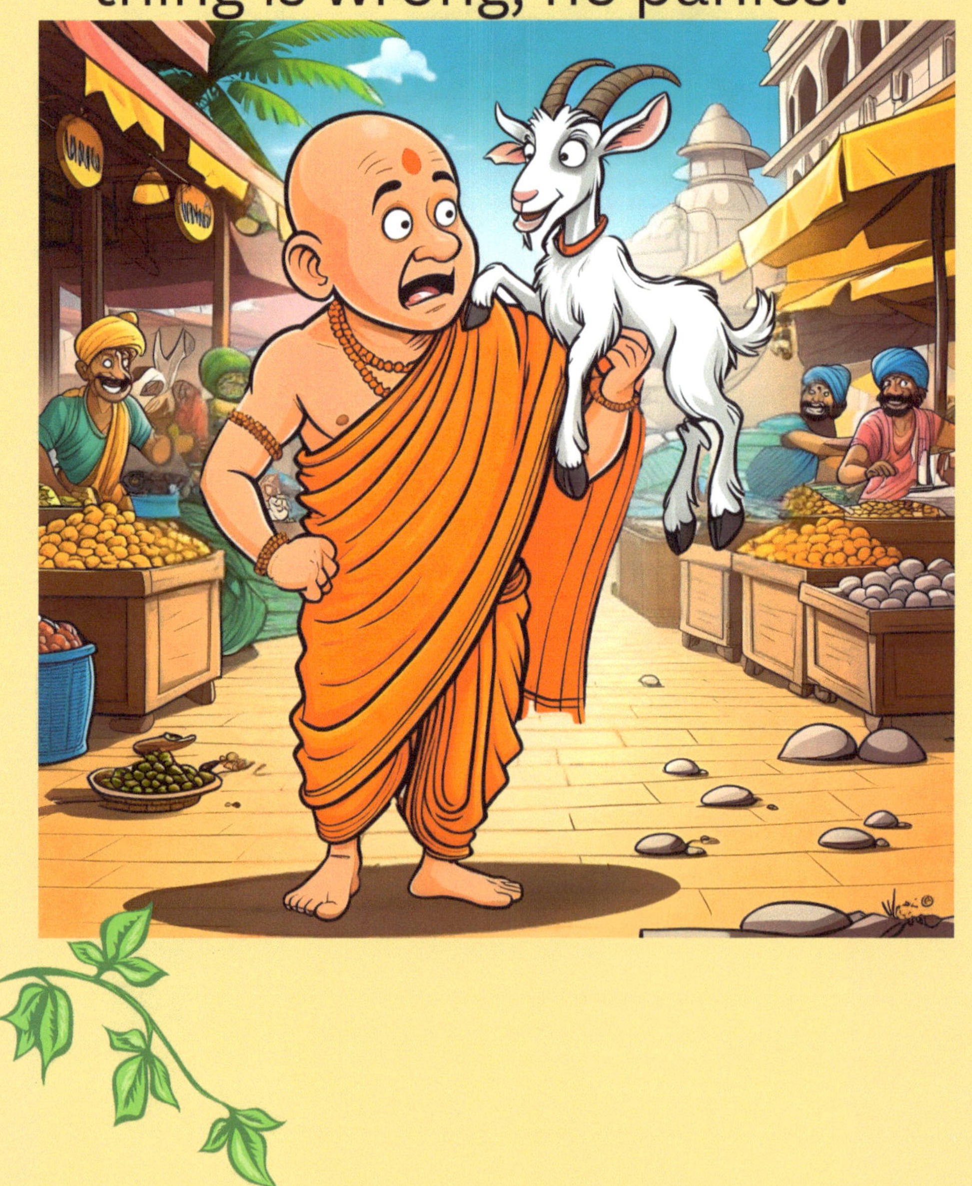

He quickly drops the goat to the ground.

And runs away leaving the goat
behind. The three thieves laugh at
his foolishness and take the goat
for themselves.

MORAL OF THE STORY

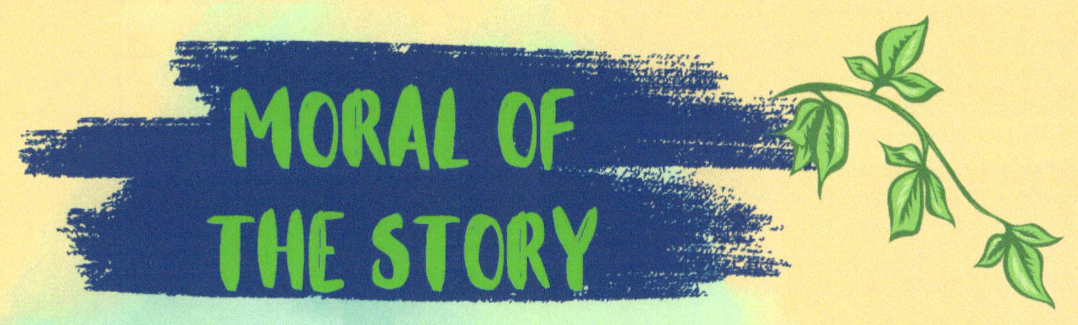

DONOT BLINDLY BELIEVE WHAT

OTHERS SAY WITHOUT THINKING FOR

YOURSELVES.

TRUST YOUR OWN JUDGEMENT

INSTEAD OF BEING MISLED BY

OTHERS

THE LION AND THE RABBIT

In a dense forest, there lived a powerful lion, who frightened all the animals.

In order to stop his daily hunt, the
animals agreed to send, one of
them as food to him, each day.

One day, it was the turn of
a little rabbit to go to the
lion. Instead of being
scared, the rabbit thinks of
a clever plan to escape the
lion.

The rabbit intentionally arrives late. When the angry lion asks for the reason, the rabbit lies, saying that another lion stopped him on the way.

The rabbit adds that another lion is challenging him and even insulted him. The lion is furious and demands to be taken to his rival.

The rabbit leads the lion to
a deep well and points at
his own reflection in the
water, saying it's the other
lion.

Enraged, the lion looks into the well and sees his own reflection.

The lion jumps into the well to attack
the other and gets drowned.

The rabbit returns safely and the forest is finally freed from the terror of the lion.

MORAL OF THE STORY

INTELLIGENCE IS

GREATER THAN

STRENGTH

THE GEESE
AND
THE TORTOISE

Once upon a time, there lived a tortoise in a small lake. He had two geese as his best friends. Every day, they talked and shared stories, near the water. They enjoyed each other's company and promised to always help one another.

One harsh summer, the lake began to dry up due to the long drought. The geese became worried. "If the lake dries up, how will you survive?" they asked the tortoise.

The tortoise sighed, realising he couldn't live without water. The geese decided to help him find a new home where water was plentyful.

The geese came up with an idea. "We will hold a strong stick in our beak and you must bite the middle of it tightly", they explained.

The Geese warned the tortoise. The tortoise eagerly agreed.

The geese held both the ends of the stick by their beaks, while the tortoise bit the middle of it. Thus they lifted the tortoise into the air. As they flew over villages carrying the tortoise, people looked up in amazement.

" Look at that ! A flying tortoise!"
people exclaimed

Hearing the people, the tortoise became happy and proud. He wanted to respond and boast about his clever friends, but the moment he opened his mouth to speak, he let go of the stick and went in a free fall.

The tortoise fell to the ground and was badly hurt. The geese were heartbroken and flew down to check on him.The tortoise, realising his own foolishness, sighed. Speaking at the wrong time brought disaster."

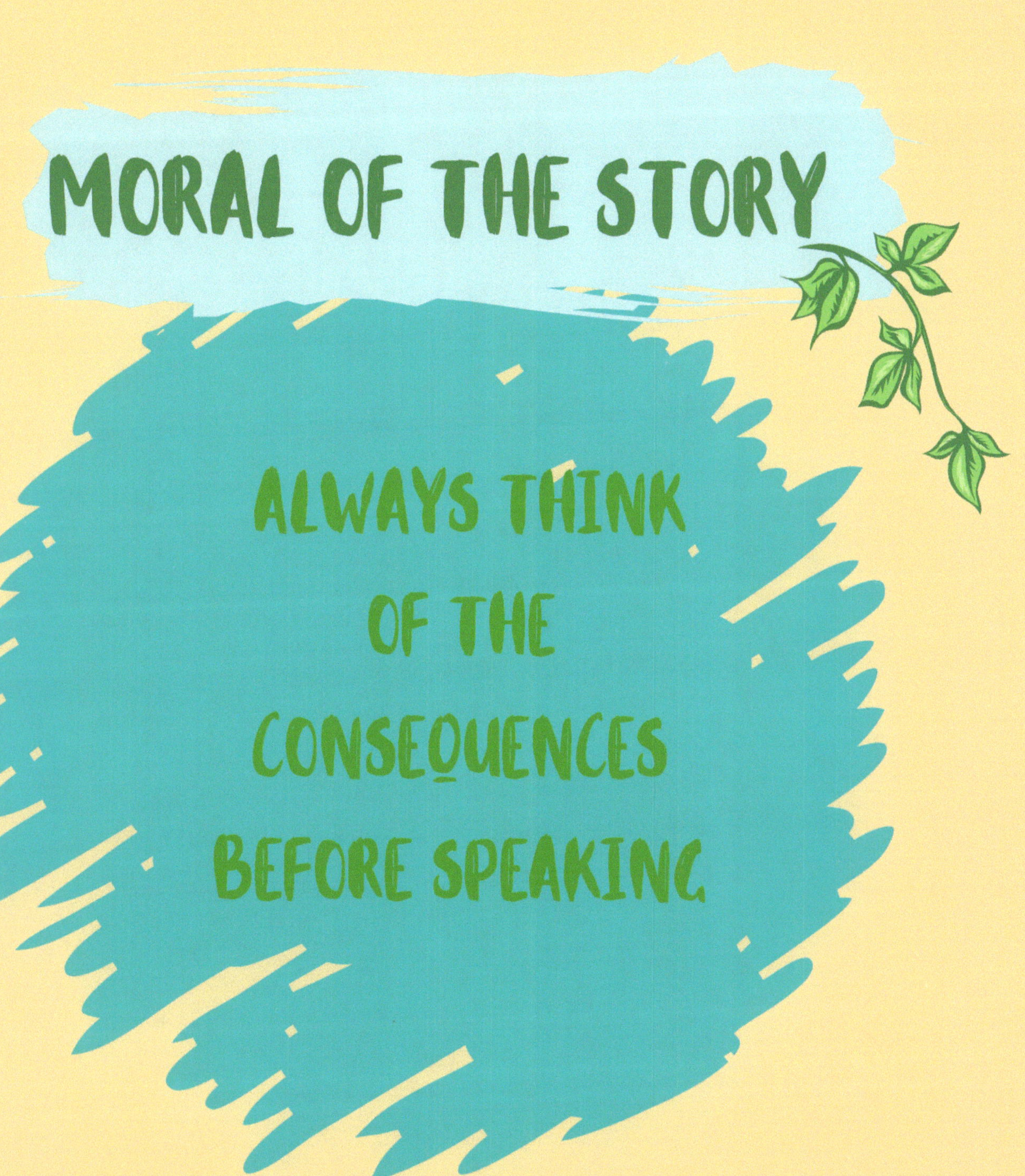
MORAL OF THE STORY
ALWAYS THINK
OF THE
CONSEQUENCES
BEFORE SPEAKING

THE ELEPHANTS AND THE MICE

In a far away jungle,
a large herd of
elephants lived
happily.

One year, a terrible drought,
dried up the rivers and lakes.

The drought forced the
elephants to search for
water, led by their wise
leader.They marched for
days, until they found a
beautiful lake, in the middle
of the forest.

Near the lake, a colony of mice,
lived in the underground
burrows.

The elephants eager to drink
and bath, stomped through the
area, unknowingly crushing,
many burrows of the mice.

The poor mice were
terrified and helpless,
as their homes were
destroyed.

The leader of the mice, a wise old mouse, gathered his friends and bravely approached the leader of the elephants.

oh mighty one, your herd is destroying our homes. Please take another path to the lake. We may be small, but one day we might be able to help you in return.

The elephant was amused. But he was kind hearted. He agreed to be careful and promised not to harm the mice again.

Days passed as the elephants and the mice continued to live peacefully.

One day a group of hunters
arrived in the forest.

The hunters set up giant traps and captured several elephants, including their leader.

The trapped elephants struggled and could'nt free themselves.

Hearing the cries of the elephants the wise old mouse and his group rushed to help their friends. Hundreds of mice gnawed at the strong ropes. Their tiny teeth worked quickly and soon the elephants were free.

The elephants were
grateful. Even the smallest
of friends can be a great
help.

From that day onwards the elephants, and the mice became the best of friends. The elephants always walked carefully around the mice home and the mice knew they could count on their big friends.

The jungle was now a place of kindness where even the smallest creatures were valued.

MORAL OF THE STORY

NO ONE IS TOO

SMALL TO HELP

AND KINDNESS IS

ALWAYS

REWARDED